MW01248547

Seeds of Laurel

Lauren Kurchak

BookLeaf
Publishing

India | USA | UK

Presentation by *BookLeaf Publishing*

Web: www.bookleafpub.com

E-mail: info@bookleafpub.com

ISBN: 9789358310016

First edition 2023

DEDICATION

I dedicate this book, "Seeds of Laurel", to my Father God for giving me the gift to express myself from the heart. I write in faith through the Spirit's heartfelt touch within me.

ACKNOWLEDGEMENT

A special, sincere, thanks to God above Who gifted me the seed of poetry to reach and touch the whole world. A word of gratitude to my friend, Emily Voorhees, who signed me up for #TheWriteAngle Writing Challenge. Finally, a big thanks to Kelsey Wilson, who has a splendid eye for detail and theme.

Time

Time means a touch in my heart to be reflecting
GOD's Presence in a heavenly atmosphere for a
devotional period to seek a new horizon and
fresh
vision while praying for my dreams to come true
as I have faith in my GOD alone.

Time means a touch in my heart to be
experiencing
GOD's special love for me as I give GOD an
ultimate,
new-found song of praise from my heart's voice
that de-
sires to be forever praiseworthy and worshipful
towards
GOD's listening ear in the heavens above.

Time means a touch in my heart to be allowing
GOD's
Spirit to probe me as I embrace His Will to make
notable
differences in the world and to be a voice of
change knowing
GOD's discipline must be involved to better my
spirit and
relationships in life.

Time means a touch in my heart to be sharing
GOD's Word
in a prayer time, as I ask the Spirit to be my
guide and influence
to enable others in accepting Jesus and to
profess the heavenly
language of the Spirit just as the Lord GOD
gives me a pure heart,
and as HE gives my world healing peace with a
message to be
"a beacon of hope" to shine beyond His
appointed lifetime!

A Whisper

A whisper calms the anxious heart

A whisper voices words of wisdom
to rule or govern in life

A whisper means for vision coming
with dreams fulfilled being from
GOD's caring Heart

A whisper causes the Spirit to be
involved as an influential guide to
bring inspiration in life

A whisper seeks to bring comfort to
a hurting, disturbed heart

A whisper loves to befriend others,
as the Holy Spirit leads the way to
redemption in Jesus Christ and for
them to be faithful in adhering to
live the Christian life.

A whisper prays to allow GOD in,
as He touches this world He created
and to bring healing at the Cross for

our hearts to bear spiritual fruit while intensely longing life to reflect, focusing on GOD's Heart!

Water

Water is such a refreshing beautiful gift of rain
from
Heaven on GOD's scenic creation

Water is such a cooling sensation after a
splendid sojourn

Water is such a majestic viewing at the horizon
of the ocean

Water is such a loving gift from GOD Who
knows the heart
and body of His Children as they seek Jesus
Who offers living
water as He can only give to His Children, as
they desire to be
in a relationship accepting Jesus' plan of
salvation into their hearts
to be born again for the vision of Heaven

Water is such a life blessing of renewal just as
GOD remembers His
covenant of the rainbow with Noah for a fresh
start after the flood

just as His Creation obeys GOD and as the Earth
humbly bows in
worship to welcome the GOD of Heaven

The Lord's Sunshine

Looking up at the skies in reflection
Seeing a rainbow of joy as GOD has given
Acknowledging His covenant life promise
and in faith between Noah and man
Cause to vow for a second chance from Heaven
And life existing after the flooding rain
The Lord's sunshine from Heaven for fruition
In giving His people blessed vision
As eyes behold the rainbow in the Lord's
sunshine
and adoringly for His creation of earth to be seen

Rainbow

Rainbow means a colorful display of the first covenant
from the heavens that's remembered always by GOD

Rainbow means a promise of hope for the world to over-
come the flood as GOD's presence is realized for His Way
through biblical history to be understood...

Rainbow means a renewed relationship with GOD for HE
cares with concern for His creation of the world in mind

Rainbow means a reflection to receive the heavenly reward
as HE gave Jesus to be welcomed into this world in order to
save and forgive all mankind

Rainbow means a lifetime abiding in faith facing the sunshine

to see His rainbow after the storms of life to just
thank GOD for
this world and for everything above the world
HE created

Rainbow means a time-sharing devotion in His
Word being grateful
to be guided and comforted by the Spirit of
GOD just as the Spirit
searches the world for hearts who will follow
and live for GOD

Rainbow means a blessing from GOD as HE
hears His children's
hearts praying to be in relationship with Him
and for allowing a rain-
bow to appear over the world as life and faith in
GOD are restored!

Ocean

The ocean is a splendid part of GOD's designed
creation
As Heaven's wind prevails on its majestic waves
in motion
And as the sun shines on the ocean to reveal a
rainbow of Heaven
Looking out the window of a plane in reflection
Thanking GOD that He walks the ocean's
shoreline with man
GOD has His reason and plan for all creation
Just as part of salvation's Cross to accept Jesus,
His Son
GOD honors humility within our hearts' emotion
Life is a vessel relating with GOD on an ocean
He's offering our hearts forgiveness as He's
Almighty GOD
that pardons and discards all sin
Making a new exploration of faith with mankind
on the Earth and ocean

When the Rain of the Spirit Falls

O GOD, my heart cries to You
Seeking Your Will, Your Word for life
Reflecting Your heart's desire for all time
May ALL the earth thirst for You
Lord, I'm interceding for this world
In uniting in faith to pray to You
As the Spirit searches our mindful hearts
ALL acknowledge You in praise
Just as Your healing wind surrounds
We abide in Your grace
When the rain of the Spirit falls

A Mountain of Time

Just to fly to a mountaintop
To reflect the scenes of nature
Walking as leaves crunch under me
As the wind blows to awaken me
The Spirit wants me to be at peace
He's taking me on a journey to be

The journey to the mountain of time
Imagine the peace of GOD there at its peak
He desires for my faith in Him to give peace
I welcome GOD alone as He's my first love
Being with Him rises me to be on a mountain of
hope
As He's my mountain of faithful grace on a
mountain of time

Imagine

Imagine what the Lord has done for me
Forever, I will sing praise in His Name
He's the One for my heart's love to breathe
I'll pray forever in Jesus' Name
Imagine what GOD has done in His time
And as time is spent to cherish nights of love
Seeking the heavenly stars as they shine above
Imagine the dream for what the Lord has done
And bless His Name within the heart of hope to
imagine

My Prayer

My prayer is not only for myself but for
the whole world to believe in a living GOD
Who loves His precious people to fulfill their
dreams as He has a plan and vision in mind

My prayer is for the world to understand the
Ways of GOD by reading His Word and for
the Spirit to guide you in life from childhood
and into adulthood, knowing GOD is your best
and faithful for life Friend

My prayer is for GOD to touch my life and heart
in a special way so I may be a witness in this
world to lead others to Jesus our precious Savior
and Lord

My prayer is for the people of this world to seek
the Spirit's Heart for living out a revival in their
land and for their hearts to experience a deep
peace that comes only from knowing GOD
Who designed relationships to be so favorably
blessed in a life-changing world....

Hope

Hope is trusting GOD to meet in
blessing with favor the needs of
daily life

Hope is having GOD move in ways
that "no one can describe or imagine"

Hope is seeing GOD work miracles
in life so the world will believe in
such a faith for dreams in Him to
prosper and come alive

Hope is believing GOD to give rest
to His People Who seek His Face to
receive comfort for worries of life

Hope is honoring GOD to forgive
offenses in life to make restitution
for a "fresh start" in relationships
throughout a lifetime

Hope is receiving GOD to heal the
body and emotional wounds of the
past as the Holy Spirit does His part
working in humbled hearts as HE

seeks the world to be redeemed in
accepting Christ their Savior for life

Hope is forgiving GOD to love life in
a new way, submitting to His anointing
as hearts of the world are seeking GOD
for His Spirit's desire just as the heaven's
rejoice with Jesus the Lamb for the world
has received eternal hope

Creation

Creation is a wonder to my eyes
As the wind calmly breezes
Seeing the waterfalls and rainbows
Walking into the aroma-filled gardens
Absorbing the scents of all the flowers
Brings serenity to my senses...

Creation pictures the beauty of nature trails
While watching nature build their nests
As GOD brings life its faithful mates

Creation reproduces and breeds as GOD intends
Knowing He provides for mankind and all
animals

Creation glorifies its life's praise to the Lord of
all heavens
Just as the sun shines to guide creation as GOD
permits
The moon shines in the starry skies to abide the
night's dreams
In reflecting the days of creation and times for
all life and seasons,
they mark new beginnings in GOD's eyes for us!

Reason

Reason loves life as GOD gives His
answer to prayers from His domain
up above

Reason attracts life to fall in love

Reason gives life a time to listen to
GOD's tender voice

Reason touches life and hearts to sing
a song of honorable praise

Reason guides life through faith in the
Spirit enjoying His Way for GOD
being our leader to overcome in life

Reason prays life for others to see
beyond a miracle while interceding
for the world to believe by receiving
salvation in honoring redemption that
heals all life (coming) in Jesus' Name

Reason shares life in caring for other
people we meet in this lifetime just as
GOD anoints for us to always shine in

this world revealing His Glorious Love
to His People, drawing all to know His
"true beacon of Hope" for His Presence
to abide in our hearts and lives as life
desires to belong with GOD forever,
"face to face," shining so emblazoned
with the Holy One!

A Bird's Nest

When you glimpse at a bird's nest
observing the work of GOD's Hand
as His beauty represented
For the egg conceived
to its hatching birth

The trees whose limbs shelter
as the Creator touches
For His eye is on the nest
He cares for the dream He created

As you awaken
hearing birds as they call to mate
The growth of wings
to soar so high
in GOD's given grace
As one heart leaves to fly
initiating the process to
make a nest

A Rainbow Promise

Just as the sun shines in the clouds
Heaven releases its rains on earth
Reflecting the day of creation
As GOD proclaimed His beginning walk with
man
In reflecting Adam and Eve
placed in the lush garden of Eden
How Satan deceived Eve into temptation
And in eating the fruit she shared with Adam
that GOD called forbidden
Facing consequences for their sin
Accepting aftermath to be forgiven
Love in GOD's heart to begin again
While remembering the story of "Noah's Ark"
GOD is faithful to the obedient, humbled heart
The raging floods from His Heaven accepts a
covenant
A rainbow promise from His heart
Permits to never abolishing by outpour floods
again to our planet Earth,
His art with love still in His heart for us
As Jesus took His cross to forgive our hearts
A rainbow glows from the Heavens
Allows a rainbow promise to praise

Beyond

Beyond means GOD's special love
from His Heart towards His people

Beyond means GOD's special time
for His Spirit to search the hearts
of those that are humble to live
serving and accepting the Christian life

Beyond means GOD's special throne
accepting angelic praise to be exalted
and hearing heartfelt prayers to solve,
as for the Lord's touch to perform a miracle
into an atmosphere that openly embraces
His favorable Presence.

Beyond means GOD's special "new" life
for His children discovering the Bible
to walk in faith by learning with the Spirit
about GOD's Son, Jesus the Lamb
which beholds "the greatest miracle" that
surpasses all:
Salvation in Jesus to be redeemed for entering in
faith
the "Heavenly realm" of life.

The Footsteps of GOD

Realizing the rain and wind is from GOD
Picturing what He created in the world
Staring out at the coastline made of sand
Imagining time walking with GOD

Following His ever present lead
Walking behind the footsteps of GOD
Treasuring the impressions of feet
on earth's ground traveled
Experiencing distance for a life lesson
learned

Learning the footsteps of GOD
Enjoying the steps of the adventure behind
Facing to explore the world of GOD
as exalted
Following Him to the beyond...

Making the journey with the footsteps of GOD
Saving us with Jesus in the land as He followed
the
footsteps of GOD present in this world

A Journey Reflects

A journey reflects the lessons from
GOD learned from life in His Word

A journey reflects salvation in the Lord

A journey reflects giving thanks for the
miracle of life as He created this world

A journey reflects Christian parents
who prayed throughout my childhood

A journey reflects my love for the Lord

A journey reflects my quiet time shared
in devotion with the Spirit to be inspired

A journey reflects as I plead to be anointed
and guided by GOD

A journey reflects spending time in the presence
of GOD to be favored at His Word

A journey reflects my will that desires the will
of
GOD by praying and interceding for miracles to
be performed as I seek the face of the Lord

GOD Means

GOD means beyond faith for His Love
to be recognized and praised for Jesus
to redeem for when GOD created the
the people of the world

GOD means beyond spiritual growth
for His Spirit to guide all who desire
His Presence into an insightful journey
to meditate in GOD's precious living
Word

GOD means beyond personal strength
as He strengthens the mind to overcome
head-on challenges and to be bold in
facing the world with faith in our GOD

GOD means beyond health for needs
to be supplied and answered through a
miracle of praying and interceding as
children of GOD knowing He cares for each
child

GOD means that our faith in Him gives me a
quiet time
so personal with realization, I'm forever freed

to be a child of GOD and as my heart honors
worshiping Him with the angels of heaven
facing the Lamb of GOD

GOD's Peace

GOD's peace shares as a fruit of the Spirit
GOD's peace lives in our hearts as the Spirit
works within and does His part
GOD's peace molds a relationship to start
GOD's peace resides and reigns in the heart
GOD's peace reasons to establish trust
GOD's peace means salvation and redemption
from the Lord Jesus Christ
GOD's peace represents "a beacon of hope"
to shine brightly to guide the troubled and lost
GOD's peace allows and permits serenity for
the weary body to enter in His rest
GOD's peace mends the broken heart
GOD's peace heals the "emotional wounds"
of the past and for our relationships to have
a "fresh start"
GOD's peace offers acceptance into His
sanctuary
for a devoted time in faith with His Spirit that's
true and heartfelt
And, GOD's peace loves "us" forever from His
Heart

GOD, Your Love

GOD, Your Love is what makes me fall in love
with Jesus in
life.

GOD, Your Love is what I focus on for You give
my life
and world such a deep peace from Your Heart to
sustain me
daily in life.

GOD, Your Love is what I always sing about to
honor You as
You favor and bless my life.

GOD, Your Love is what makes my heart
devoted, as I desire
Your Spirit with me to reflect "the Bible" and
scriptural devotions
reserved for a quiet meditation time spent as one
in life.

GOD, Your Love is what opens my heart to pray
to You and to
receive the anointing You established while
being receptive to

Your Call upon my life...

GOD, Your Love is what lives within me to lead others in a
prayer time designed to welcome the Spirit's Presence to dwell in
this intercession of seeking Jesus to "redeem all life" just as I give a
prayer of thanksgiving for the greatest miracle of souls in this world
receiving salvation and surrendering to GOD by living ways for the
redemption reward of eternal life!